Embers Of The Soul

Alka Singh

BookLeaf Publishing

India | USA | UK

Made with ❤ on the BookLeaf Publishing Platform

www.bookleafpub.in

www.bookleafpub.com

Dedication

For seekers and soul searchers

May you find light...

Preface

Acknowledgements

My sincere thanks to Bookleaf Publishing for creating this opportunity.
My sincere thanks to my family and friends for all their support and encouragement.

1. Ballad of Love

My love,
How distant you stand?
Disgruntled and disowning?
Don't look away,
Don't retract
For only death can decree parting
And untie us to new paths
Of rediscoveries
Of renewed vowing
Of rebirth

I remember a day
When I came to meet you
You enraptured my senses
And held them hostage forever
In the sound of the infant's first cry
In the illumination of daylight
In the smell of odourless oxygen
In the taste of mother's milk
And in the engulfing warmth of human touch

You smiled,
You let me believe-

I was your princess,
I was your beloved
I was your betrothed
I grew, I aspired
I surrendered to your mysticism
As I danced away
Like the graceful smoke leaving the earthen lamp
I soaked in the color-bursts
Of blue skies
Of green fields
Of golden days
And of silver nights
I remained starry-eyed
Drowning in your hazel eyes
Your lashes fluttered my sparrow-heart
And I lost myself to music,
To a Thornbird's piercing song

My love,
But were you holding my hand when I fell?
I refuse to believe that you may have let me go
Oh! My brazen heart
Oh! My perfervid soul
Oh! My blinded senses
Why did you not learn to read-

The niggling greys
The smell of flesh
The sight of blood
The claw of nails
Digging deeply into your free spirit
Oh! My absorbed senses
Rise from your slumber
Or, on second thoughts,
Rather remain in it
For all that exists outside
Is a frightening graveled pit
Where roving echo-locating bats
Are out to prey
To detect their sense-objects

No, never,
Don't ever come back to your senses
Such that you can never go back to naivety
In the realization of betrayal
Of your world
Of your beloved
For the finger you so lovingly hold on to
Is nothing true
But a figment of your vibrant imagination
An excerpt of your deranging illusion

2. The Circle

I'd been looking around for years
When all I had to do
Was look a-round
Why? It was always there
The insight...
In the earth
In the sun
In the moon
In the orbits
And even in the construct-the wheel
All motion is in rotation
In revolutions
Of the circle, in circles
The circle of life
For a circle stands not by itself
But only when it remains in motion
...in journey
So there you are
Alight on it...on life
But keep moving to stay...to exist
For that is the only meaning to it
The rest!?
Moving images that come and go
To a sum of nothingness

The sacred absolute
The transcendent zero
So it is-another circle...   5
Encompassing the circle of life

3. Pilgrimage

It was this ritual walk
Uphill along the oaks
That had driven my years of mortality
At the summit sat my God
Just at the end of the darkness of pines
Into a space where earth met the sky
Through interspersed valleys sublime
There he sat, the God, the shepherd
Watching ardently...his flock
His eyes drooped in weariness
The lines on his face...deep caverns
And I thought each held a story
And it made him laugh at my naivety...

Each sheep passing by...
He said in retrospect
Was a part of his life...yester moments
I asked him to show me the path
Tell me how battles die
And every time he said
"Go live..." for the story is not yours
But you are the story in the universe's manuscript

"Go live..." he said
For life it is, the very redemption of itself
For life it is, in annihilation of each day
That it moves to new shores, renewing itself...
For life it is, that in all its impermanence
Gives you the eternity you seek

4. Prisoner's Tale

In lavishing endowments
Nature chose man for the most beautiful
The beautiful mind
To seek the truth
To see beyond
The passage of thoughts and emotions
To essentially realize
That which is
And that which is not
As one and the same
Ah! But for the moment
When it gets caught in anchorage
And starts spinning ecstasy
With its serrated claws
The spider-mind
It choses ego as its center
And hence can spin the radius,
The limiting insight
It spins around
Frame after frame
Connecting, intersecting
Definitions of image,

False weight, achievements
Or mere baits of fleeting falsities
Of exaggerated atrocities
Till it feels caged
In its own prison pit
Coated with a stickiness
That pulls it back, the spider-mind
Into its own spit
Ah! Nature pities
Oh! For the wretched mind
If only you valued your freedom
To venture beyond
Would you have not remained beautiful?
Would you have nor realized the beautiful?
The truth of truths
The only truth-
That you exist
Beyond establishment
Beyond definition
As life, in life
Infinitely

5. Soulmate

The precincts of the solitary riverbed
The dark moving waters
They are the witnesses tonight...
As we celebrate our oneness
Our wedlock
You say, "Let us be one,"
"Let me listen to the rhythm of your heart"
...and it sounds like a serenade
To my numbed senses
Intoxicated by the strong winds
In delirium, I lead you to the boat by the river
Leaving behind footprints on the sand
Telling of a time when it stood still
Overpowered by myth
And the timelessness of my impassioned soul
We meet
You feel for my contours
I long for immersion
You hunger
I linger
Gaping holes in the boat
Allow waters to invade

Threatening to wipe out our microcosm
You panic for life
I smile at death
You resist, you float
I accept, I sink
You feel for my heart
You aim for the surface
I remain embedded in your soul
I dwell in the depths
You are the heart
I am the soul
Oh! So entwined, not ever lone
Oh! So entwined but no, never one

6. Conversation of My Heart

You are the solitude of my heart
The isolated vastness...
Where all the commotion is in its silent emptiness
The only conversation of my heart

The incompleteness runs amok
Like a moth caught between four walls
But the only direction availed
Is that of burning down...
In the hope of the lonely flicker
That of the diminishing flame
The only conversation of my heart

The deadly stillness
Carries a disquiet
Conjured by the fracas of your insipid heart
And seismic responses in mine
In the epicenter of nostalgia and longing
The only conversation of my heart

For when you know it
And you cannot help being it

And its incomprehension that drives
You follow your own ghosts
Into cobwebs, dark pits, and vortices
Shrouded in mystery
The only conversation of my heart

I speak, I listen...
But I never let go
The incessant conversation...
I keep away, I indulge
For love is the only conversation
But never do I comprehend this madness
For comprehension is merely rhetorical death
Of the endless conversation of my heart

7. Remnant Soul

Entwined like two creepers
Torn apart by their paths
Of different roots and different skies
Yet remaining...
We meet invariably, incompletely
I chide every moment
That digs deep into my being
That defines my existence
With only yours in it

Time is a clown
For it cannot be corrected
And it laughs as it sweeps me by
With every tick with you in it
I try hatred for a burdening lie
I try giving you away
I try wiping you out
Denigrating you as the fumes of rising senses
But all you do is stay
And rise within my spirit
Neither as destination
Nor as a milestone

But in your sheer non-existence
So persistent like irreplaceable vacuum
And so you come
And go...
But never go
Like a remnant of my lost soul
Yet again searching for me

8. Hara-kiri

My alter-ego sneers at me
My shadow laughs at me
My reflection pities me
My conscience loathes me
I'm searching a way out of myself
I'm looking for myself
I try recalling a day when I could have lost myself
A day I enslaved myself
To mental constructs
To obnoxious percepts
Repenting the day I established myself in a race
Where I chose to stand above all else in place

There must have been a day
When I stopped asking, "Who am I?"
There must have been a day
When I evaded answers to, "Who am I?"
But the memory's lost
The context's lost
And all I retain

Are fossil remains
Blows of amputated limbs
Wild gushes of bitterness
A bottled-up stature
A life without harness
Such is the strife of a self-obsessed heart
Held captive by a self-created contort
Such is the loneliness of a self-centered heart
Held captive in a self-created fort
I remain the only viewer
Of the ugly exhibition of my life
I remain the only archeologist
Trying to figure out the debris of my life

9. Solely Yours

In all your unpredictability
In your distasteful wrath
In your overpowering fury
In soothing winds
I know you give,
You only give
For you, I stand unexacting
Like the fisherman by the sea
The net in his hands
That will pick up matter
And fill it with soul,
His very own
Unseeing through a metric
Unperturbed, trusting
He lets the salty waves crush him
Keeps standing in penance, and therefore still stands
Feeling washed
Feeling blessed
Feeling loved
Feeling owned
By the sea

10. Tender Feet

Tender feet,
Don't hurry to sound words
Lest the empty stickiness of their syrup
May spin a web around you
And you lose the music around you

Tender feet, walk away
Turn away before the tendons tighten
That may tie you down
And make you captive in the castle of myth
And you remain from building castles in the air

Tender feet, don't close doors
Until you've seen the rainbow
Let it enchant your soul,
May you breathe in the prism droplet
Such that the colors remain with you

Tender feet, don't give away your ears
To resounding echoes
To the frantic calls from behind
Go, run little one

Run alone
Run free
For only these magic years are your own
The rest to come, are but only sins to atone

11. Pursuit of Destiny

Tired of watching the endless trail of sin
I summoned the absolute within
I asked in desperation of finding the truth
I asked amidst the commotion-
"What is this unending pursuit?
What is this conversation-less motion?
What would the ants achieve after all-
Anything more than a summer evening?
And when would humans finally arrive-
But to a finish line of counted breathing?
Then what is all the noise about
If the reachable cannot be drawn or sealed
And all that seems attainable after all
Is just one of an infinite layer, an outer onion peel?
The mirage called destiny
Is but a rotating wheel
You think you've reached, you think you'll reach
But by then the end-post has lost its feel
The wheel has traveled further down
With a new restlessness in sight
And if you think you've ever possessed a crown,
It is yet again a vacant spot-its vulnerability impatient to

reveal

How far would one pursue this dream
That never loses sight
How far would one travel the path,
And never halt to smile
Every goal has a name, a face
That withers away with time
So where do I, all my efforts expend
If my life after all is not so prime?
The inner voice holds my hand
Helps me climb atop the wheel
Tells me destiny is not material gross
But immaterial joy across
It is the journey that is to be lived each day
No future, no past, no plans in play
So travel along, and in communion
With compassion as your companion
For no human mind is larger than life
That, nevertheless, sustains itself without unwanted
strife
All that matter of importance is just science renewed
Of convertible energy, a theory reviewed
In the name of pursuit and all that was ever there,
Never created, destructed, never requiring your prayer
So let go of ruthless driven-ness, let go of hedonistic
pursuit

Let go of the illusion of 'my life' and its fruits
Let go of all Brownian motion, the churning of the
transactional loom
For all that unnecessary doing, undoing simply leads to
entropic doom

12. Water Body

I was born as a brook
Delighting in gurgling innocence
I played my way through mountains pure and friendly
pebbles
Ferns and unknown defense
I met a few ponds on the way
Halted as they called by
To let me feel the warmth of homes
Hiding between weeds, the snails, fishes, and little fry
I thought I'd stay but there I go
It's just not me to dwell
For my spirits call me out in the wild
Invoking a zeal that never quells
I joined streams and rivulets
But never the serene of the lakes
For I thought the stagnant lotus-blinded top
Never lets your soul awake
Here I was- ripe and young,
Mesmerized by the serpent's moves
And surrendered unabashedly
To a dancing seductress' groove
"It is the elixir of life", she said

"The life within life"
She carried me away to unknown banks
Never letting me step outside, never in the insides of
strife
I've never stopped moving yet
Caught between flooding and eroding
Have I forgotten how to establish existence in flux
That I continue devastating or depriving?
I stand at the threshold where oceans meet
Intimidated by its expanse
I've never stopped moving yet
But in an indecisive resistance
The oceans rise to swallow me
I shudder at the sight of swelling death
I hear the enchantress' hollow laugh again
At my ignominy that cost my breath
A voice tells me to let it all go
And let the overwhelming take it all away
Accept the end of motion and restlessness
Embroiled in the light of day
A voice tells me to let it all go
And let the overwhelming take it away
Accept that there is a greater calm
When you rest eternally in night's bay

13. The Banyan Tree

"How can you keep standing,
And never feel stirred within?
How can you even claim to live,
And never give up or give in?"
Ah, yes! I'm over a few hundreds,
And the Lord made me a Banyan
Ah, yes! My life's been an Odyssey
Every second defiant, every pain an eon
"How would one know,
If you've ever met one?
How would one know,
If you've ever stepped out of your prison?"
My longevity is my truth, my character
Not a choice, not calibrated defense
But yes, the Lord has been kind enough
For the branches he gave, rooted in resilience
I've seen it all here,
In my canopy, dynasties lost and found
I've heard it all here,
Cries of inconsolable lovers, quick to rebound
I've seen every emotion encircle me
Through a defined path

Of a material something to an immaterial nothing
Like attaining the immortal soul through mortal wrath
I've seen every action equalized
By a quintessential duality
And have known little that the earth is about
The rotating day and night, and its infinity
Thereby I stand in quietude
To tell you how to live
To stand unperturbed but with fortitude
Never to ask but only to give
You'll know you've lived only if you let it pass
As the abundant flow of life
You'll know you've lived only if you let it pass
Without ever longing for it, this barren life

14. The Buddha

There he goes, in the orange robe
His shadow trailing forever
He has crossed mountains and seas
And now he crosses my threshold
I try to still my restless eyes
In the puddle between his legs
So sure he'll leave behind footprints
Which I can follow for eternity
But no! He walks on and on
Never a mark to leave
And exasperated in my clouded heart,
Lost and abandoned I feel
Where is the path I was to take?
Where do I go from here?
For I haven't counted the stars above
And I don't really want to reach there
I come back to my enclosure
Look deeply at my reflected face
Holding intense creases of stormy weather
And the fatigue of beaten bricks
But when calm descends on the mirror
A benign warmth envelopes me

And tender words of *The Buddha* flow
And echo within my soul
"Don't borrow footprints and treaded lanes,
The script is not for you to read,
The truth is yours,
The path ever yours,
So carve it with your feet
This journey is from self to self
The rest are loops between
So don't dwell in here, move on my child,
Unravel your destiny
But hold a hand wherever you can,
Never the grip of your own grasp
Kiss the earth in such a way
That it exudes fragrance all around
Go! Lose your joyous heart and head,
Never fear to give in love
But warily take what is only yours
That in essence is what life gives
Don't knot your stay in ties and webs
Don't breathe in shallow relief
But spread around like the peaceful water and wind,
Happy, unbound and free"

15. Lotus

Here I am, out to fathom this world
As fickle as the eclipsing binary
Oh! So full of life
Oh! So dark with death
And I think I see both
And I regret I saw none...
It is not the world out there
It is the blind spot within
Which never lets me see the inside
Which never lets me see the outside
Which never lets me perceive
That I am the world
And the world is I
That all otherness is a myth
In the root of 'I'

So 'I' let 'you' be my mirror
Reflecting all ebullition
In underpinnings of
Envy
Pride
Desire

Greed

So that I can see the ugliness of the froth

So that I can feel the dirt on my porcelain face

And not just wipe it away in disgust

But let it transform within

To flower beyond 'otherness'

To flower beyond 'I'

Like the Lotus in bloom

Which knows not of an existence

-of exquisite beauty as 'I'

-of muddy waters as the 'other'

16. Sunshine

Deep fascination woos me
As I watch the sun go down
It's not easy for the sun
To conceal its effulgence
And let the night take over
Take its prime

The night tries taking a stand
By putting forth starry glitter
But all that comes through
Is the mighty effort to radiate
Simply borrowed sunshine

I too think of a sun
That shines through my darkness
And let me majestically be
A king in my smallness
I swell, I rise
I dwell in lies
I believe the glitz

Think it's all mine
But when I tire
And it's dawn
I start fading on my own
I start surrendering to a supreme
For I cannot restrain-
The light from emerging
For I cannot contain-
The truth from converging

17. Truth

-

Is there reason to build...?
To establish...?
In what's already established?
Is there reason to make efforts,
To come into one's true nature,
To come into one with this universe,
To come back into harmony and blending,
To come back to where one began,
And needs to walk back?

The truth lies in what is...the coordinate
Not in speculations of what can
Concocted by the groveled pit of desire
So waiting to take you up by storm
In its cyclonic winds
Far away to places where you'll never find yourself
...or the truth

Tread on to find your path
In the purification of spirit
In the surrendering of putrefaction

Led by illusions of existence
This is it...all to be rendered
To be replenished
As the only truth
That of quiet existence...
That of inwardness...
That of equilibrium...
As the art of being

18. The dry leaf

Another hour has slipped by
A handful of time wasted
A reach repeatedly extended
And there it stretches again
My hour of becoming
Trapped in human frailties

I look at the dry leaf falling
Envying its equilibrium
As it gently sways to balance
The imposed speed by gravity
I wonder if I'm less porous
Or attached by too many strings
To be unable to remain integral
In this bipolar plane
I wonder if it is a matter of time
Or if I'm merely an object of time
To be unable to establish significant minutes
On the clock hanging on someone else's wall

The dry leaf touches dust
And to dust it returns

Then how am I any different
If simply matter in an urn?
I wonder if there's more to life
Than material concerns and pursuits
I wonder if I can organically be
Like wiry tendrils around unreadable silhouettes
How I envy the dry leaf
That has known life in its essence
How I hate every tick of the second
That rules my mindful presence

19. The Permanence of your Love

When my philandering thoughts are chained to you,
All I seek is surrender
I despise the violent rising of desire
Condemn the dehiscent pores
That ooze the unannounced amber of honey
When your shadow falls on mine
 But I allow you to bruise me
As you walk away without detaching the chain
For I still believe that you will complete me
With the permanence of your love

The blue monarch flutters by
And I feel the tickle under my eye
I wonder if you are breathing so close
And I wonder if I'm imbecile
You stall my every move
As my revolting body defies
Every dogma
Every constitution
Every tie
To believe that one lie

That you will –when you will- complete me
With the permanence of your love

I keep tracing parallel worlds
Drawing endless lines
I reject differences that never meet
Pretend not to see the truth on the decline
I'm preserving a disaster
Like a mind clouded with wrong science
For the earth was never flat
And infinity never found
But there again goes a crippled belief
That you will –a day will come when you will- complete me
With the permanence of your love

20. Exclusively Ours

You remain adamant as ever
You still occupy the inescapable corner of my mind
I remain adamant as ever
I still rant invasion of an abominable kind
You part ways, choosing a new life
I part ways, choosing an old life
We turn away
We come away
We vow never to return
We disallow desires to scald and burn
But what about a crossroad
The map has long been laid
For exclusively ours is the node
And like cymbals in our life
The intersection ever plays

You said you always lost
I said I never gained
Exclusively ours is the frost
Exclusively ours the ripening wounds
You speak of incessant blame
I speak of wrongdoing

Exclusively ours is the accusation
Exclusively ours the horizon-less conversation
That searches each other as a friend or fiend
That much as we try, it never ends
Hence-
Exclusively ours is the knot
That never unties
Exclusively ours is a love
That never fills, yet never dies

21. Impressions

Beginning a child's play
I picked up some clay
Moulded it as my mind
And played a game of casts and binds
But a storm came by
Made me a dune
And my impressionable mind lay bare
Open to all communes
You were grazing sheep
Looking out for green pastures
And I thought you were the shepherd
Protecting vulnerable creatures
You playfully laid your hand on the dune
And I absorbed it as a caress
You lay down to rest on the grass beside
And I latched on to you with a harness
The dunes now carry impressions
Resembling the waves in your hair
The dunes have now turned to stone
Waiting for a new repertoire
The mind, once mine, wanders encased
Drowned in the myth of entrenched lines

And sighs as it lives on in myth
Burdened by falsities in deeper confines
The mind contemplates why you still impress as an
anchor
And not as a flirtatious trespasser
The mind exasperates as you still validate the mindless
stupor
Holding an astounding myth as 'you' within a greater
myth as 'I' – still waiting for closure

22. In Search of Love

If 'ours' was a myth
Every hour was a myth
You and I, the 'us' and 'we,'
The very togetherness was a myth

We did not last
We could never have lasted
For we held on to crutches
To support broken legs

The bones got back in place
The sun got better,
You ran into blazing sunlight
I hid in darkness

Ah! The hearts,
It just slipped our mind,
That which we promised to agglutinate,
In the forever of our breath

So were you ever searching me?
And I, ever you?

Were we the answers to each other?
Or questions we now refute?

45

No, it is not about you or me anymore
But only the love we seek
That lives and is eternal ever more
In the crave of lovers, requited or bereaved

23. Shadow Lover

I drag myself from lodging
Every time I look into your eyes
And feel the pain of uprooting
From a beautiful homeland

I curse my blooming nerves
Every time you evoke my senses
And feel the pain of detaching
A severed arm from the torso

I chide my engaged moments
That remain –forever- entrapped by you
And feel the parching of dry land
Thirsting endlessly for rain

You bear a shunned existence
In my glorified conscience
But you remain all essence of experience
In the realm of imagined presence

You are true in every pain
But never the joy of truth

And in this very negation
You have established your ambiguous revelation

47

Because-
You were,
You are,
You will ever be,
In all virtual reality
In essence and waves
In shadows and reflections
In formlessness
In senselessness
Thereby-
In eternal oneness

24. Mask

No, I don't look up
While I walk amongst
The sea of people trudging along
For I know they are masked,
Just like me...
In a peel of completeness
A futile act of conformity
Don't ask me...
Even I cannot show the crater within
Erupting though...
Brimming...I wonder if it's only me
...only my heart
Etched in deformity
Ensconced in volcanic glow
So I look into your eyes again
To see in it, my mirrored soul
And find that it is the human trough
Merely waiting for the crest to rise
And I understand that the plateau in show
Equanimity - is universal myth
For it is unevenness
That makes us grow

The completeness lies
In the incompleteness of it
So let it come –
-pain
-agony
-despair
Let it come to slowly lift you
Let it be with you when it comes
Let it come to slowly lift you
To fairer seasons through the tears
Let it come to slowly teach you
The extraordinariness of the ordinary
Let it come to gracefully impart
The beautiful experience of being human

25. The Rising Storm

You are the tempest of my mind
Or the tumult of the heart
You're the enraging rise of desire
Like the whirlwinds in my dream
You are what I never seek
You are what I never surrender
You are...but what rises to storm
Invariably in my being
Ah! But a dream...
Where I still let the softness of my mind
Play against the soles of my feet
Dancing in the swerves of passion
Unperturbed by the rising of it
In the garb of a storm
I move to your rhythm
Smiling through it all
I'm up in flames
Soaked in desire
I'm looking for a release
To speak the seamless
The language of exploration
In poetic wildernesses...

For it is when I know deep inside
It is the avalanche of desire
It is the rising of the storm...

It is not for me to catch the wind
Or let it draw me in its vortex
But to let it all pass by,
Let go...
And yet remain...
For that is the essential existence of calm
Even within the rising of the storm

26. Jigsaw

The many autumns passed by
Both breezy and stormy
But I left not my axis
And my addictive game
-the jigsaw puzzle

There were years I spent
Playing with tact
And reveling in a supposed fact
That within me resided
The genius, the God

But when the years strolled by
And the puzzle pieces
Lay bare and with frayed edges
So much like my life
I gave it up in form
But remained addicted in my mind
-the game-board now my life

Disowning misery, I drooped
Alone in the park an autumn evening

Gazing at dry leaves in chaos
I remained caught in the stillness of dust
But as the dust settled one on another
Preparing the trees to spring again
Within me dawned the essence of the game
Of a greater harmony
Within the disharmony

So now I let the autumn be
For it no longer is a myopic game
-the jigsaw I so tried to arrange
But it is the harbinger
Of the cuckoo about to sing
Of the spring about to come

27. Oneness of Humanity

The last conversation I heard
Was that between man and his nation...
Was it a feud??...as is always??
The contention usual –
That of ownership and protection
Typically, of who protects whom–
The man, the nation?
The nation, the man?
A faction intervened
Said why? None?
Futile...I say
The clashing of swords
The worlds on fire
Rivers of blood
And all that we claim to save
Senseless...I say,
The grief,
The strife,
The thumping of hearts
All hollow causes...pocket beliefs
Have dug a dark pit of death
For in the purposelessness

Of vocabulary, verbosity, and paradigm
We have but forgotten a simple expression-
A single word
To build a single world
The oneness of humanity
That envelops all,
That protects all,
That owns all,
Holding together beads in a string
In the oneness of harmony
Above individuals
Above societies
Above religions
Above nations

28. Downpour and the droplet of time

There is a black cable
Which I perceive without ends
As the continuity of life
The garland of time

I sit quietly
Watching the downpour
Through my window
My eyes remain arrested
By the trickling of water droplets
Beautifully falling off the string of time
Some solitary
Some in unison
Like the perfect and imperfect moments of life

The downpour descends
Creating thunder, lightning
Floods, puddles...
Fury, wrath
And yet...quenching it all
The parchedness

With its bounty

So I see, it is this and that
All and none
The dance and the downpour
The rain of life
Incessantly true
And so I see,
The trickling droplets
The continuous moments
Moments of time
Each trying to hold its own
Establishing itself
Signifying itself
As the truth in the chaotic lie
The roaring downpour of life

29. Seas that don't meet

She is that rudderless boat
Caught in the ocean's storm
Washed over by the intense waves
Tossed to ephemeral water whims
But never brought to the shore

Broken and bruised, she laments
"Why have you rowed me so far?
When you know not your own shores?
Why have you drifted with me?
...with such aimless abandon?"

There were shores once,
The termites sucked her
The crabsters holed her
But when the waters came
They clung to her
They owned her, called her home

But it was this ethereal fisherman
Who unanchored her stealthily
And made her wander after him

Promising new abysses of ecstasy
Only to take her out
And leave her in that rift of dereliction
In the ocean of depth
That has no boundaries
But to separate...
Be that chord of destiny
That disallow yearning seas to meet

Now as she sinks slowly in fragments
To a cold stillness below
Her heart is a bubble of loneliness
Trapped in the labyrinth of unfinding
As she drowns in the dark shelves of desire
All she can barely gasp is-
"Why fisherman...?"
"Why me...?"

30. Solitude, come home

The heaviness of a hot summer evening descends on me
A weary film covers me
And like the tortoise, I quietly contract into my solitude
Undoing corrugations on my face
By rippling moods
And replacing it with a monastic calm

It is easier now to let the loitering heart swing
It is easier now to contain the noise and converse
It is easier now to caress old wounds
And in my solitude, it is easier now
To not let my human be capsized in the whirlwind
Of lust, ambition and amassment
Come home now, solitude...
Let us celebrate homecoming today...tomorrow
For the rest of my life
Let me flow like an inconsequential stream
Gurgling in solitude
Flowing along
Without bruising myself
By the rocks that must stand where they do

Like the myriad events and turns in my life

31. Usurper

If life is time,
You've devoured it entirely
With your stubborn existence
Etched in absence

If my mind is water
You remain dissolved
Threatening its very characteristic
Even in invisible solubility

I despise being a captive
I long for my freedom
I long so much for my own existence
Now totally usurped by you

I'm fading away
Like the light at dusk
The dark canopy of illusion
Enfolding me such
As if I no more remain
Without you in my eyes

Without you in my words
Without you in my breath

32. The Human Kind

You're not human-
If you don't carry a hollow globe of discontent in your head
And it's burdening weight in your heart

You're not human-
If you yearn to hold a dislodging hand
And feel stifled by an enclosing hand

You're not human-
If your happiness is not salted with tears
And your despair clothed with an insufficient smile

You're not human-
If you're knowingly suffering an else's inadequacies
And unknowingly throwing your own all around

You're not human-
If you're not drowning the world with falsities
And swimming desperately to find your own truth

You're not human-

If it is loneliness you so detest and fear
And then go back to solitude as the only refuge

65

You're not human...No! You're not-
If it is the human kind you're devastating
Only by being a lesser, insufficient human

33. Bubbles

What if we are bubbles-
Enclosed in lifetimes encircling on different planes
On a spiral of time
Meeting, un-meeting each other
Pricking, poking or dancing in enchanted whorls
Around each other
Under the spell of our fantasies and illusionments

What if we are bubbles-
Mere prisoners,
Sometimes listening distractedly, more often deaf
To the yearning scream for a release from within
A call to redeem
From endless strife, bloodless battles
From incomprehension of conflict and chaos

What if we are bubbles-
Our existence, the biggest lie we're telling ourselves
What if bliss is beyond this captivating froth
Of mad pursuit of one thing or the other
What if it is all there, what we seek
Waiting for us to burst open the bubble

And blend seamlessly into eternal freedom

67

34. New Poem

www.ingramcontent.com/pod-product-compliance
Lightning Source LLC
LaVergne TN
LVHW051228200726
843510LV00011B/1518